GW00481995

BEFORE
THE
FROST

HEATHER GODDIN

BEFORE
THE
FROST

Heather Goddin

Copyright © 2016 Heather Goddin

The moral right of the author has been asserted.

Apart from any fair dealing for the purposes of research or private study,
or criticism or review, as permitted under the Copyright, Designs and Patents
Act 1988, this publication may only be reproduced, stored or transmitted, in
any form or by any means, with the prior permission in writing of the
publishers, or in the case of reprographic reproduction in accordance with
the terms of licences issued by the Copyright Licensing Agency. Enquiries
concerning reproduction outside those terms should be sent to the publishers.

Matador
9 Priory Business Park,
Wistow Road, Kibworth Beauchamp,
Leicestershire. LE8 0RX
Tel: 0116 279 2299
Email: books@troubador.co.uk
Web: www.troubador.co.uk/matador
Twitter: @matadorbooks

ISBN 978 1785890 987

British Library Cataloguing in Publication Data.
A catalogue record for this book is available from the British Library.

Printed and bound in the UK by TJ International, Padstow, Cornwall
Typeset in 11pt Minion Pro by Troubador Publishing Ltd, Leicester, UK

Matador is an imprint of Troubador Publishing Ltd

For Christer

Before the Frost

Out of the blue,
Sudden and unsought,
These last bright days of summer
Before the autumn frost
Late flowering love
That transforms winter into spring.

Yes, I am old. I am old
But when we are together
I am young. I am young.

SINGER

When I was young I sang:
Sang for myself and sang for the world.
In the breathless, quiet seconds before the applause
I knew if the audience were moved.
The longer the silence, the greater my joy
And I carried the world
In the palm of my hand.

Now, when I would sing to you
I am mute. The voice is nearly gone.
I paint in words
What once I gave in song.
But if my poems move you,
As my songs might once have done,
Then I carry the world
In the palm of my hand.

Toe in the Water

I stand here up to my knees,
Water still rising,
Out in mid stream
Willing you to come.

I watch you dip your toe in the water
And I smile, knowing you will come.
Step by careful step,
Ankle, shin and knee
Until we stand together
Face to face.

But whether we will swim together
I do not know
For only time will tell.

Coup de Foudre

I never wanted to love again
But I reckoned without the *coup de foudre*,
The lightning strike, the thunderbolt
That knocked me off my feet.

All I wanted was a quiet life.
Comfort, contentment, the company of friends.
No more this madness of the heart,
This crisis of the soul.

But you are the top brick in the chimney,
The apple in the crown of the tree
Which is why I am chasing rainbows
And crying for the moon.

Schwartzwalder Kirschtorte

As the coach toiled on upward
Through forest and meadows
Somebody cried, "It's a long way to come
For a small piece of cake!"
At each hairpin bend somebody groaned
But the views from the top were well worth the climb.

In the inn at the head of the pass
When they served up the cake,
All voices fell silent,
Amazed at the size of the slice.
We ploughed our way through the luscious concoction
Layers of cream, kirsch-sodden cake
And decadent cherries steeped in liqueur.

Sated we sat for the cake demonstration.
Oceans of cream, buckets of chocolate,
Whipping and grating,
Smoothing and shaping,
The tilting of bottles, the topping with cherries.
Then rounds of applause
For the cake-makers' art.

Then back to the coach, undoing buttons, loosening belts,
All weighing more than on the ascent.
The heavier coach seemed to travel much faster
The sun shone much brighter
Our hearts felt much lighter
Remembering the taste of the Black Forest Cake.

We were shown how to make it
To pass on to others
But might need a mortgage to do so.
Two litres of cream, the very best chocolate
Not counting the bottle of kirsch.
Too much of a good thing might pile on the weight
But we'll never forget the Schwartzwalder cake.

For Those Who Wait

I, who never weep, am weeping now.
The hidden tears that no one sees.
For the wastage of years and days
When life is all too short
And time is what we do not have.

I weep for lack of you, for need of you.
Your smile, your touch, your warmth.
The very beating heart of you.
I wait to see your writing on an envelope.
I wait to hear your voice.
Conjuring up substance from the thought of you.

I weep through bitter arctic winds,
In freezing snow at sunset light.
On empty frozen starlit nights
My time with you too far away
To even count the days.

MIND AND HEART

Now, when I would run to you
I would waddle in ungainly fashion.
If we embraced, my spectacles would clash with yours.
I may not always hear the words you say
And in some moment of love's gentle bliss
I might get cramp
And fall upon my face.

But mind and heart have no infirmities.
My thoughts can fly to you
By day or night.
And if we kissed
My crazy heart would dance.

VINTAGE WINE

Sitting beside you, drinking you in,
It seems to me that you are like fine vintage wine
Seasoned in oak,
Great clarity and depth.
An excellent bouquet
And smooth upon the palate.

Not everyday drinking
But something quite special
To lay down for a lifetime
And savour through the years.
A wine of which I never tire.
A very fine vintage.
A very good year.

SEVENTEEN

I look at you and see
The tall, slim, red-haired boy
I never knew.
And then I look again and see
The gentle man you have become.

My mirror shows me
What I do not want to see.
Where did she go,
The girl that once was me?
But when we meet the years recede
And I am only seventeen.

BREAKFAST WITH CHRISTER

Each day in the freshness of morning
We gather up cutlery.
Make our selections from meats and from cheese,
With newly baked rolls.
Count out our pills
To take with our juice or our tea.
But the star of the show
Is the jar full of honey
From which we dip freely
Taking turns daily to lick out the spoon.

Into my mind comes the rhyme from my childhood
From *Winnie the Pooh*:
'Isn't it funny
How bears like honey!'

So what does that make you and I,
Dear Christerbjörn?

"Björn" (Bear)

FLYING

I walked with you through crowded streets
When every step meant pain.
But I was happy to be there with you
Laughing and talking on our way.

We passed young lovers strolling in the sun
"How nice," you said, "to see them hand in hand."
And how I wished that you and I
Would one day do the same.

Then yesterday you took my hand.
We walked like that through crowded streets
And in my joy I never noticed pain.
It seemed to me my feet had wings.
I felt as though I flew.

SHIP AGROUND

Sometimes I feel like a ship aground,
Stuck fast in mud.
Waiting for the tide to turn
To float me off to join the other ships
Far out at sea.

Yet here I am, still grounded on the shore,
Too deep in mud to ever sail again.
My crew abandoned ship,
Took all the cargo from my hold,
My home port ever out of reach.

Here I have company of sorts
The other rotting hulks around the bay
All waiting for the miracle
That makes us whole again.
To feel the movement of the sea beneath our keels
Amongst the other ships on open sea

BLACKBIRD

Sleepless, I rise an hour before the dawn
And go in search of tea or Ovaltine.
Far to the east the faintest gleam of light.
The fading moon, now at the fall,
Hangs tangled in the branches of the wild plum tree
Turning its myriad blossoms into snow.
The garden sleeps in monochrome.
The night is not yet day.

The silent village slumbers on.
Too early yet for lorries or for cars.
I warm my frozen fingers around my mug
And listen to the silent world.
Then comes a small, sweet ripple of sound,
So soft I hardly hear it 'til it comes again.
A sliver of song in the silence
Becoming a ribbon of sound
That grows in volume and in beauty.
The blackbird, leader of the orchestra,
Practising his notes before the other birds join in.

Listening to his glorious song,
I am soothed, uplifted and inspired.
High in the branches of the Judas tree
Sings feathered joy.
Harbinger of spring.

'Comfort me with Apples'

It's raining again, of course…
What shall I do today?
Chinese New Year.
I'll catch the bus to town and shop
Take advantage of the offer
On Chinese nosh.
More than enough for one
But if I'm careful
It will do me twice.
I can have a little feast
All on my own.

I buy my Chinese food and scour the shelves for other things.
Now, shall I buy a Yum-Yum or a Lardy Cake?
No, better not, I've bought a pudding for tonight.
I'll have a coffee on my Waitrose card.
There might be someone there I know
And if there's not
Then I can sit and watch the world go by.

What shall I do this afternoon?
Write a letter or a poem,
Ring a friend (who won't be there),
Watch some rubbish on TV,
Until its time to eat.
Whilst my meal cooks I'll light all my candles,
Have a glass or two of wine
And raise a toast to absent friends.

What shall I do tomorrow?
If it's fine I'll catch the bus
Have a coffee somewhere nice
And walk beside the sea, perhaps
Until its time to catch the bus back home.

But what if it rains again?
I should have bought that Yum-Yum!

JULDAG (CHRISTMAS DAY)

I think of you going out into the dark and bitter cold.
Driving on empty roads to a ferry.
Crossing the icy seas and wintry isles
To reach a small place on the edge of that distant archipelago.
To take a Christmas service.
All to keep a little church alive.
It is an act of dedicated faith and love.

And then, I think of that other night
So long ago, when it all began.
I think of the Magi and of shepherds
Following a star.
And I wonder if on dark seas, perhaps
Or walking through the trees to the chapel
You look up to the moonless canopy of stars
And think, too, of that other time,
Following your own bright star.

My thoughts fly to that little church.
I see candlelight, feel human warmth.
I hear the age-old message of the Christ Child's birth.
I see fellowship, the company of friends.
I see sunlight on winter seas and frozen earth
And I know that with those there
You will be filled with peace and joy.

But, I think, too, of the weary journey back
And I want to send you warmth and light
To keep you company on lonely roads.
But I do not think you need them.
On stormy seas, in biting cold,
In wind and rain or driving snow
God's love and strength lie in your heart
To bring you safely home.

MYSELF WHEN YOUNG

I found a photograph.
Myself when young.
So innocent, so vulnerable,
Dreaming my dreams.
And I feel like a grandmother,
Wanting to warn of the perils ahead.

But would I have listened,
Taken the advice?
I truly doubt it,
And if I had done so
I would never have taken
The tortuous path with its twists and its turns
That led me to you.

TREE

In youth we think we have
The monopoly on love.
Blinded by beauty, lust and desire
We do not always see the tree
For what it truly is.
Our eyes see only the brilliance of leaf and flower.
We lose our way in the forest,
Blundering around, in love with love.
Making mistakes,
We cannot always see
The wood for the trees.

But as the days grow short
And yellow leaves begin to fall,
We start to see the shape of the tree
Without its springtime glory.
We see its strength and grace
Its wounds and deformities.
We see the truth of it
And love it for itself.
The way through the wood is clearer now.
Perhaps we could call it wisdom
But it is love nevertheless.

Birds

I have known parrots and jackdaws
Even the odd bird of paradise,
Robins and plenty of sparrows
An owl or two
And once upon a time, a heron.

What bird would I choose for you?
No question in my mind.
The skylark, resting on the ground
But always soaring heavenwards
Singing its glorious song.

So what am I?
Something much smaller, a wren perhaps,
Its voice quite out of proportion
To its size.
Or am I, more chillingly, the nightingale
Tearing its breast against the thorns?
Needing the pain to sing.

NOW

When we are young we feel immortal.
Life stretches out for us
Endless and full of hope.
Plenty of time to live our dreams.

Let us, in age, forget the future.
There is too little time.
Let us, for a short while
Make the past recede.
The only surety we have, is now.

Let us not waste this moment,
Cast it aside or throw it to the winds.
For this could be
The last time that we meet.
Let us then laugh and talk
Of everything and nothing.
Capture for a moment
The reality of dreams.

CUL-DE-SAC

I am well aware
That this road leads to nowhere.
A cul-de-sac.

But the view is beautiful
Even at a distance.
And if I can go no further
It has to be enough.

When my steps begin to falter
And my sight begins to dim
Let me just sit here and focus my eyes on dreams
And the roads that take me where I want to be.

As light fades
And the night grows cold
May the last thing that I see
Be a canopy of stars.

IN YOUTH AND AGE

When I was young I knew a German girl,
Drowning in floods of unrequited love,
Who wept on my shoulder and piteously cried,
"I want to be old and all this is past
And loving is over and done
When life will be calm and serene".

She found her happiness
With somebody else.
Passed out of my life.
But I think of her sometimes
And hope that in age, if she is alive,
She has found all the things that she most desired
And life is now calm and serene.

But how could we have known, either of us,
That love's no respecter of age?
Still causes torment and pain.
Maybe it's worse, when there is so little time
To get it right.

I hold out no hope
For calm and serenity.

TOYBOX

He, who holds us in thrall,
The Enchanter,
Keeps us like toys in a box
Each in our own compartment.

Then, one by one, he takes us out,
And we, the enchanted, the bewitched,
Dance, play and sing for his delight
Until it pleases him to put us back
And let another take our place.

But woe betide the one who out of turn
Tries to climb out of the box.
"Enough is enough" he says,
"Get back in the box."

The others know their place
But I, alas, do not.

SECOND FIDDLE

Looking back, it seems to me,
I have played second fiddle all my life.
Second to a wife or someone's sons,
Someone's friend or someone's Cause.
Always the bridesmaid or the runner-up.
Never quite good enough.

Maybe I tried too hard,
Sprinted ahead, ran out of steam.
Got pushed aside by others in the race
And never reached my goal.

Perhaps I was too lazy,
Never tried hard enough.
Lacked that streak of ruthlessness
And let another take my place.

Now I am old and growing tired of life
It doesn't seem to matter any more.
But I wish that you would listen
To the music that I make for you.

It is second to none.

Loving and Giving

Forgive me if I'm wrong
But I always thought that Christmas
Was all about loving and giving
For did not God the Father
Give us the greatest gift of all.
His son?

Christmas is the time when we give gifts.
Not for gain but as our thanks
For kindness given
Through the year.

Did you think I sought to *buy* you
By giving you a gift?
And if you thought it merchandise,
I really couldn't afford the price
You've put upon yourself.

Whatever happened, I wonder,
To the season of goodwill?

IN A BAKERY

Looking around at all these goodies
I think I know what your problem is,
You want your cake and you want to eat it.

I wonder if you know
How lucky you are.
I don't think I've ever had my cake
Let alone been able to eat it.
Most of the time I just get bread,
Occasionally a scone or a bun
And then I am grateful
To get a bit of butter on it.

COUNTING IN URDU

They sat beside me in a small café
In a sleepy Suffolk town.
Two old ladies with a little dog.
Extraordinary hats.
One white and floppy with a wavy brim
The other like a man's.
A high-peaked cap with multi-coloured studs
Just above the brim.

Memsahibs, wrinkled by a fiercer sun than this,
In cut-glass accents, talked of childhood in the Raj.
I sat with my coffee filling in time
And eavesdropped on their talk.

"Can you still count in Urdu?"
"I'm not quite sure. Shall we try?"
And they solemnly counted up to ten.
"I remember the soldiers," said one.
"I was very young.
One gave me a button from his tunic,
I have it still."
And her companion said,
"Well, fancy that!"
And all the time, the little dog
Circled the tables, trawling for crumbs.

They paid their bill
Put the dachshund on its lead
And left.
The café seemed less colourful
When they had gone.

FOUR LOVES

From love of the sea
It was inevitable
That I would love, not one
But two sailors.

From love of an island
It was inevitable
That love for an islander
Would rise from it.

This time it is different.
From loving a man
I have come to love his country,
Learning what shaped him.
And whatever comes of our friendship
I will never lose my love of the place.

MALTA IN WINTER

'Almond blossom, oxalis, acanthus,
Artichokes and masses of oranges.'

A few words on a postcard from a friend.
Nostalgic, evocative
Making me homesick for a place I love.

I loved it long ago.
I loved it for its innocence,
Chaotic and unique.
I loved it through its years
Of turbulence and strife.
I watched it leap decades
To reach this century too soon.

Now, brash and modern
With its veneer of sophistication,
Almost, but not quite, like everywhere else
I love it still.

Like loving someone, seeing their faults
And loving them even more,
So Malta is for me.

But some things never change. Thank God.
Almond blossom, oxalis, acanthus,
Artichokes and masses of oranges.

CRANES

Sometimes when I am limping along
You tease me, smiling, saying,
"Why don't you jump? Come on, just jump!"
When we both know well I couldn't
Even if I tried.

There is a marsh in Sweden
Where the cranes will come to breed
At the end of their springtime odyssey.
Three thousand miles and more,
Crossing the seas and continents
Against all odds.

Soon the unattached young males
Seek out a female of their choice
And dance to curry favour in her eyes.
Leaping and dancing, higher and higher
Until she joins him in the dance.
And then the others all join in,
Noisily giving thanks.

How I long to see this place
And watch the springtide dance of cranes.
At journey's end, so joyous and so beautiful.
Maybe there I might find strength
To jump for joy myself
Like the migrating cranes.

Who knows, with lessons from the cranes
When next we meet
I might be able to jump.

RAGAMUFFIN HEART

Love, here is my ragamuffin heart.
It's been around a bit.
More than one careless owner.
Battered and bruised,
Scratched and scarred,
Scruffy at the edges.

It needs a good home.
If you will take care of it
It will repay you with its dog-like devotion
And love you all the days of its life.

HAPPINESS

Pleasure is a warm room on a cold, wet day.
A good meal and a glass of wine.
Familiar writing on an envelope.
An unexpected call from distant friends.
Music and laughter. The sunshine after rain.
A smile from a stranger in the street.
The company of friends.

Joy is the sun in winter.
The first green buds of spring.
A flight of geese across a clear blue sky.
The sight of distant mountains and a turquoise sea
Fringed by a white sand shore.
It is the scent of a rose. A summer breeze,
A Beethoven sonata, stunningly performed.

But happiness is you.
From the moment that we meet,
Your smile, your voice,
The firm clasp of your hand.
Shared laughter and the chemistry between us.
Happiness, pleasure and joy
All in one place.
My happiness is you.

Vännen Min

Sometimes you are my father,
My anchor and my rock,
There to protect and guide
Showing me, by example,
The way to live my life

Sometimes you are my child,
In need of comfort or encouragement,
And as mothers do, with love,
I try to lift the darkness from your heart
And let the sunlight in.

But most of all you are my friend.
The person that I know and trust
Who likes me for myself, despite my faults.
The one I can tell anything and everything,
Who makes me happy just by being there.
For whom I would lay down my life
If there were need.
My almost-lover, vännen min,
My friend.

Vännen Min – My friend

COFFEE AND CAKES

I think of her often,
Your long dead wife,
Knocking on the door of your study
With coffee and cakes.
Wanting your attention.
Needing the comfort of your love.

Am I so different?
Knocking on the door of your heart?
Seeking to amuse you
With my letters and poems,
Willing you to think of me.
Wanting the comfort of your love.

I feel for her
And believe that she would feel for me too
(Sometimes I sense her near)
But you always opened the door to her.
She always had your love
And I am glad of it.

And I?
However hard I knock
It falls on deaf ears
And the door stays shut.

HODMADODS

Early each morning, my neighbours' cat
Comes pounding on my door, demanding milk.
Uttering pathetic cries, muddy ginger paws upon the glass
But often he rejects the milk.
Not to his taste or slightly off?
But by morning it is always gone
A hedgehog, fox, another cat
Or maybe he came back within the night
And finished it?

The other night as darkness fell,
Reflected kitchen light
Showed two black blobs upon the plate.
Torchlight revealed two hodmadods
Side by side siphoning up the milk.
Next morning all was gone.
No need to wash the dish?

I looked again last night and there they were.
Not two but five unlikely guests.
Not milk this time but cream.
My night time entertainment:
Milk-fed snails.

Hodmadods – Old Suffolk name for snails

FAIRY STORY

If you asked me to go
To the ends of the earth to do your bidding
I would not return empty-handed.

If you asked me for the stars
I would pluck the diamonds from black velvet skies
Enough to fill your hands.

If you asked me for the moon
I would bow and wish, then swing the new moon low
To shine on you alone.

If you asked me for my life
I would lay it humbly at your feet
To do with what you will.

But if you asked me for my heart
There would be then no need.
It is already yours.

La Dolce Vita

In the days we are together
We live like lords.
Good food, fine wines, glasses of champagne
And I am always happy to share it all with you.

But when the money peters out
And we can't afford the cost
I'll settle for a *fika* (coffee and some cake?)
Or *Dagens Rätt*
(An *Isterband* or scrambled egg?)
One glass of wine, perhaps?
And I shall be happy
Just to share it all with you.

Fika – The Swedes' favourite 'anytime' snack. (Usually coffee and cake.)
Dagens Rätt – Dish of the Day. (The cheap lunchtime option.)
Isterband – a delicious smoked sausage, eaten hot.

METAPHYSICS

I think of the things
My father told me
Of the science of reality.

"How can we prove we're here?" said I.
"There is no proof
For this could be a dream within a dream," he said.
And I, the child, would always say,
"But if you pinched me and it hurt
Then surely *that* is proof?"
But now I know
That pain is often there in dreams
And we can wake and never know
Its cause or whence it came.
A dream within a dream?

But, oh, the greatest mystery of all.
What when the irresistible force
Meets the immovable object?
Neither will give way.
If I am the former and you are the latter,
I think that we will cling
Fast to each other in futile embrace
Into the mists of time.

HOPE

My spirit knows it well.
The feathered steed on which it rides.
The small, frail bird of hope.

Mostly, we fly quietly
Just below the clouds
Fixing our gaze on a distant star.

But sometimes hope soars,
Goes out of control,
And my spirit reins it back
Before it plunges earthwards
Where the deadly chasms yawn.
For then, with all its strength,
My spirit has to drive it up
Away from the abyss.
Back to its careful height.

The star still keeps its distance
As we fly quietly on,
Below the clouds,
Through daylight and through night.
My spirit and the small, immortal bird
Called hope.

CLOSE TO HEAVEN

Sometimes, on a bus or in the theatre
You suddenly drop your guard
And lay your arm across my shoulders.
Love moves through me in a warm, gold flood
And I want to turn my head to kiss your cheek
But I don't quite dare.

Sometimes, at a concert, when we listen to music
I look at your hands lying at your side
And I want to slip my hand in yours
To share what moves us both
But I have been hurt too much in the past
And I don't quite dare.

But sometimes, when we are alone
I dare to lay my head against your arm.
Then your arm will come around me
And for a second you will lay your head on mine.
From the core of love inside me
There rises the bitter-sweet thought
That this is the closest to heaven
That I shall ever be.

PLAIN FACTS

"I've seven funerals," you said,
"It is too much."
It is indeed too much.
Your prime obligation is to your Parish
But the private ones are something else.
I see the horns of your dilemma.
By saying 'yes' to all the rest.
You are the man who can't say 'no.'

But do they see, those relatives and friends
Who want you, so much, to fold away their dead
How old and tired you are?
They see what they want to see,
Your dedicated, willing heart.
You knowingly put your head in the noose.
You do it for love.

When you begin your own eternal sleep
Who then, will they ask?
They'll have to settle for another priest.
Not, perhaps, their choice.
In matters of death and disposal
No one's indispensible.

From afar I watch you burn yourself out,
Unable to slow your all-consuming conflagration.
So who will take *your* funeral?
However much you want to
It certainly won't be you.

NUCLEAR WINTER

If I should lose you
The sun would tumble out of sight,
The stars would shatter into dust,
The moon swim out of orbit.
This would be my nuclear winter
When black rain fell from an ebony sky.

For you, death is but a doorway to another life.
For me, of lesser faith, my only wish
Is to die before you do.
For how could I survive
Without your light to guide me on my way,
Your hand to lead me though the dark?

Departure

I never watch you walk away.
After what seems eternity
I hear the door click shut
And you are gone.

I sit on my balcony
Waiting for my transfer to Arlanda,
Seeing the brilliance of light on water.
The seagulls resting on the thermals
Under a clear blue sky
And I listen one last time
To the bells of the German church
Playing the noonday hymn.

If only I had access to seven-league boots
Or the Genie's magic carpet
Instead of sitting here with a breaking heart.
I want to be gone.

WAITING TIME

Now I can count the days
On the fingers of one hand.
The waiting time is nearly done.

Then, for a little time
I shall be happy
But the precious days will flow out
Swiftly through my fingers.
Gone in a flash.

Soon I shall be back
To the months and weeks of waiting time.
The way it has always been.
The story of my life.

The Tower

A river lies between us, holding us apart.
Sadly, I never learnt to swim
Or row a boat.
In the unlikely event that you wanted to reach me,
If you tried to swim across
You would drown.
Pulled down by the weight of your armour.

You have built yourself an impregnable tower
On the opposite shore.
Made of strong brick and impermeable stone,
Built to withstand every siege and assault.
You have bolted and barred every window and door.

Sometimes you open a window
Inviting me in
But if I grew wings
To travel across
You would reach for your bow and your arrows
And shoot me down.

Prinz Eugen's Waldemarsudde

On a day full of sunshine
We climbed from the tram
And took the winding path
Through parkland filled with flowering trees,
Weird and puzzling modern sculptures,
Lawns sloping to the water's edge.
All around the vibrant green of springtime
Sunlight sparkling on the sea.

We climbed the hill to the house,
Poised above its terraces and lawns.
Its rooms were light and spacious
With their treasures of paintings and works of art.
The memories of a gracious past.
A house that had been loved and cherished.

"I could live here," I said with delight
And you agreed it would be nice
To live in such a house
But said you'd need a staff to cope with it.
I said, " You could have one half
And I'd have the other
With a room in-between
Where we could sometimes meet."

You said,
"I'd keep my door locked."
I said,
"Mine would always be open
But it would be nice
If you knocked on it first."
Such are the games that grown-up children play.

Prinz Eugen's Waldermarsudde. The nineteenth century home of *Prinz Eugen,*
artist and art patron. Now one of Stockholm's favourite museums

ENCOUNTER IN DUNDEE

On the cusp of the year I walked along the waterfront.
Ahead of me in the middle of a bridge
A man sat, muffled up against the cold
Of a damp, dark Scottish winter.

What I saw was despair.
Total and utter despair.
No outstretched hand,
No pleading voice,
Only a handful of coins
In a cap in front of him
And silence.

I passed him by and then, on impulse,
Turned back and threw some coins
Into the almost empty cap.
He murmured thanks.
"Do you have to do this?" I said.
He raised his eyes to mine.
"At the moment, yes.
They offered me a place in a hostel
But I couldn't... I couldn't."
And then I saw the pride as well as the pain.

He wasn't old but neither was he young.
A mass of dark red hair.
A thick and curly beard.
A cultured voice,
An old, thick double-breasted overcoat
And quite incongruously
A small, neat holdall at his side.

Never, these days, very steady on my feet
I nearly lost my balance.
Up came his hands to steady me.
"Oh please don't fall," he said
And I saw kindness and compassion
Written on his face.

I wished him luck and went on my way
But the memory still troubles me.
I wish now I had emptied my purse of coins
Into that little dark cap.
Maybe I was afraid he might have spent it
On drink or drugs.
(Could one have blamed him?)
But he smelt of neither,
Only despair.

For some strange reason
The memory haunts me still.
I wonder what had brought him so low
And how he fared in the long, dark winter up ahead.
I shall never know the outcome.

WATCHING AND WAITING

Each night, I watch the moon grow bigger
From the windows of the dining room.
I sit amongst the living dead.
The sad, old, silent, lonely men.
The even sadder women on their own
Who sometimes smile but seldom speak.
The couples who don't speak at all
Not even to each other.

Tonight out on the roof top terrace
A ramblers group sit with their drinks.
Take flashlight photos of each other,
Vying with the city lights
And lightning flashes out to sea.
They make their speeches, raise their toasts
Then all troop out in single file
To find another place to dine.

Tomorrow will be different.
You will be here to light the gloomy room
Breathe life into the vacuum.
And all I have to do
Is wait a little longer.

DÉJÀ VU

We walked to the bus stop
Slowly, arm in arm.
You, with your stick on the left
I, with mine on the right.
Propping each other up
Like a pair of bookends.

Out of the crowd came a little old man.
Silver-haired but spry,
Elegantly dressed and smiling.
He came and stood in from of us,
Looked from you to me
Beamed at us and spoke.
"What is the road to heaven?" he said.

Too surprised to speak
We smiled, said nothing.
"Love," he said and was gone,
Still smiling, into the crowd.
What did he see in us
Or *think* he saw?
We went on our way.
Neither of us mentioned it.

But this has happened before, I thought
You and I, in this very same place,
Same time of day
With the same old man and the words he said.
But I knew that it had not.
I have heard of this and read of it
But never known it until now.

Déjà vu?

The Man from Santa Venera

The Rabat bus was full
Only two seats left.
One beside a fat young man
Who overflowed his seat.
The other with a thin old man,
Singing to himself.
Plenty of room for me.

"You've a lovely singing voice," I said.
Brown as a nut and wrinkled like a prune,
He turned to me and smiled,
White teeth flashing in the sun,
"When shall we get wed?" he said.
"Not in *this* life," said I.

But all the way to Santa Venera
He sang to me
Elvis, the Beatles, love songs of his youth.
When he left the whole bus rocked with mirth
And so did I.

But…how often is one honoured
By an offer of marriage
From a stranger on a bus?

Not very often
And only in Malta, I think.

OCTOBER SUNSHINE

I sit in the lobby
Waiting for you to come.
Looking out on leaden skies and driving rain.
I watch you stepping from the bus
Solemn-faced beneath the umbrella.
Collar up against the rain.

You climb the hotel steps.
I make no move
Just watching you.
Wanting to hold this memory to myself
For just a little while.

And then you raise your head at sight of me
And smile, like sunshine through the rain
Chasing the clouds away.

In this moment I know that whatever the weather
This will be a lovely day.

AIR CONDITIONING

The Maltese night was hot.
The restaurant was new, the food was good.
We sat the four of us
And talked of this and that
Laughed and joked together
As old friends do.

The air conditioning was good.
In my case, far too good.
Sleeveless, low-necked, I sat and froze
Caught in its full and icy blast.

Why did I say nothing?
Perhaps I thought they felt it too.
I watched the food cool on my plate
Drank my ice-chilled wine,
Being the stoic that I often am.

We finished our meal
Sat and sipped our wine.
At last I said, "I am so cold."
Gave you my frozen hand.
Quick as a flash you rose
Put your jacket round my shoulders,
Filled with your body's warmth.
I felt as though your arms encircled me.

If I hadn't already been in love with you
I'd have fallen in love with you then.

THE TRIP TO VAXHOLM

The City was *en fete*.
The last of summer, unseasonably warm.
We boarded the steamer,
The oldest in the fleet.
A miracle of polished wood and burnished brass.

The ship was full.
I wondered just how many it would hold.
We found a space on deck.
In front of us, along the rail
A line of rucksacks, jeans and bums.
Not much chance to see the isles,
Too many people at the rail.
Just now and then we caught a glimpse
Of passing boats, of sea and trees.
We held a competition, just the two of us
To choose the neatest bum,
You liked one and I preferred another.
Could not agree on whom to give the prize.

The space we had was small,
Not really big enough for two.
Your arm went round me
Holding me close.
Much closer than we'd ever been before.
My senses swam from love of you.

I felt the long, slow, sensual movements
Of your fingers on my arm.
Circling my elbow, caressing the skin.
Love surged through me like the tide
And flowed from me to you.
I laid my head above your heart
Within your circling arm.
Did you notice what I felt?
I doubt I'll ever know.
But for a while you leaned your head on mine.
I wished that we could stay that way
Until the end of time.

But nothing lasts for ever,
We reached the quay and disembarked.
We ate a lovely lunch, herring with lingon,
And from the windows of the dining room
We watched the world go by.
Sunlight glinting on the sea.
Water taxis, sailing ships and pleasure craft.
We ate ice cream in warm September sun
Walked amongst the crowds
Then took the ferry home.

Plenty of room this time for both of us
To watch the islands gliding past.
The yachts, the ferries and the tourist boats.
The places that we know and love.
We sat together but apart
Companionably close
But your guard was back in place.

In the long, dark, lonely days ahead
When I am missing you,
I shall remember Vaxholm.

SLIPPERY SLOPE

Why did we have to meet so late,
When both of us
Are on the slippery slope
Struggling to keep our feet?

So many things I would have shared with you
And there are many things, I think,
You could have shared with me.
We could have done so many things together
Had there been time.

But what is the use
Of regretting all that might have been
And all that cannot be.
Knowing that had we been young
It might have been called love.

So, I will concentrate instead
On these few lovely days
I spend with you
And live each happy, shining day
As though it were my last.

A TERMINAL INSANITY

Knowing what I feel for you
(torn between pleasure and embarrassment),
You sometimes say,
"You are completely mad!"
I think I would agree with you.
It is a terminal insanity.

Acknowledgements

My grateful thanks to Celia Rhys-Evans, who valiantly printed out the poems for me; to the friends who urged me to publish them; and to Blake Morrison, who sourced Matador for me and encouraged me to go ahead.